I0126476

# 9 Keys to Successful Audits

## Denise Robitaille

Paton

PROFESSIONAL

Chico, California

Copyright © 2014 by Denise Robitaille.

All rights reserved. No part of this publication may be reproduced, distributed or transmitted in any form or by any means, including photocopying, recording, or other electronic or mechanical methods, without the prior written permission of the publisher, except in the case of brief quotations embodied in critical reviews and certain other noncommercial uses permitted by copyright law. For permission requests, write to the publisher, addressed "Attention: Permissions Coordinator," at the address below.

Paton Professional
P.O. Box 44
Chico, CA  95927-0044
*www.patonprofessional.com*

Ordering Information
Quantity sales. Special discounts are available on quantity purchases by corporations, associations, and others. For details, contact the "Special Sales Department" at the address above.

9 Keys to Successful Audits/Denise Robitaille—1st ed.
ISBN 978-1-932828-68-9

# Contents

# A Reliable Assessment Tool

Internal auditing is one of the elements that makes your quality management system complete. It fits snugly into the "check" component of your plan-do-check-act cycle. Internal auditing isn't a haphazard or optional occurrence that you tolerate to maintain certification. It's an assessment tool that provides a reliable indicator of the integrity of your organization's system and processes and their capacity to support your goals.

The purpose of audits is three-fold:

- To assess and confirm conformance to defined requirements
- To determine the effectiveness of processes and the quality management system
- To identify the need to initiate correction, corrective action, and/or preventive action.

Audits should result in:

- Fulfillment of customer requirements
- Continued certification to the ISO standard (or sector-specific equivalent)
- Improvements

Audits help you to identify problems, risks, good practices, and opportunities to better serve your customers. The information garnered from well-conducted audits is an asset that far outweighs the modest investment in time and training. The manner in which the organization values and uses this asset is partially dependent on how audits are performed.

Executive management, through visible support and allocation of resources, has the primary responsibility for ensuring the effectiveness of the internal audit program. Auditors have the responsibility for utilizing good auditing practices, conducting thorough and conscientious assessments, and producing meaningful audit reports. The person in charge of the internal auditing program is responsible for managing all aspects of the process and for ensuring the effectiveness of the internal audits. For supplier audits, these activities are often managed by or done in conjunction with the purchasing function. For certification bodies, regulatory agencies, and other third parties, the responsibility for various activities is parceled out to administrative functions in conjunction with any other effected groups in their organizations. All the players have the mandate to provide valuable information that management can utilize for strategic planning, supplier qualification, certification, and/or other decision making.

What follows are some of the practices that will help your organization reap benefits from its auditing program. Although the comments are directed primarily at the first-party (or internal) audit, most of the tips are equally valid for second- and third-party audits.

# CHAPTER 1

# Plan and Prepare

O ne of the most undervalued practices for ensuring the effectiveness of an audit program is the consistent development of good
audit plans. Just as with any other process, the planning that precedes deployment is a reliable portent of the quality of the output.

It doesn't matter if it's a first-, second-, or third-party audit. There are
common factors to consider. The audit plan has to take into account various constraints, including the size and layout of the facility, time, individual schedules, and the general availability of process owners. This has
to be weighed against the need to ensure verification of fulfillment of requirements that are indicative of the effectiveness of individual processes
and ultimately the whole quality management system (QMS). In short,
you have X number of things you have to check in a defined period of
time to conduct a fair, balanced, and creditable audit and arrive at your
conclusion.

The single best reason to have a plan and to communicate it is so that
people know in advance when you'll be in their area. It's common courtesy. This goes a long way toward dispelling the witch-hunt mentality
with which people usually perceive the arrival of an auditor. Failing to
alert process owners of planned audits carries other negative consequences. They already look upon the audit with the dread of suspected
felons, even though they've done nothing wrong. As long as individuals
believe that an audit is a surprise attack designed to catch them in error,

they won't look upon the audit as a fact-finding event designed to foster a culture of improvement. Problems are covered up out of fear of punitive action, resulting in cyclical repetition of errors affecting product, performance, and the bottom line. There will be more discussion on the need to allay fear in chapter 2.

Efficiency is another reason for having an audit plan. It saves time. The auditor has a sequence that makes the audit flow smoothly and logically from input to output through a series of processes. Effective planning brings an element of "lean" to the auditing process. It minimizes the backtracking and repeat visits to areas that eat up precious time without adding value. Time lost in redoing activities and in extra travel time has been identified as "waste" that has a detrimental effect on the bottom line.

For internal audits, there are two distinct forms of planning that occur. One is the planning of the entire audit program for a defined cycle—say one year. This is usually encapsulated in the audit schedule. The other is the preparation that precedes each individual audit.

## Audit program

There are many factors that go into the development of the annual audit plan. Addressing them properly increases both effectiveness and efficiency.

I had occasion several years ago to work with a quality manager who was implementing an ISO 9001-compliant system. Having completed the training of the internal auditors, I turned my attention to the individual who would have responsibility for managing the audit program and for facilitating individual internal audit plans for his teams. He had opted for quarterly audits of the whole system, utilizing three auditors who would perform the assessment over a two-day period. After giving him a few pointers, I left. The next day I got a call from my frustrated and exhausted colleague. "This audit planning stuff is hard," he whined. "I've been at this for over three hours." It takes time to develop a good audit program. But once it's put together, the audits run more smoothly and the output of the audits has greater value.

# Frequency

Most management system standards (such as ISO 9001) require development of a plan of audits at determined intervals. This means putting together a schedule. The chief factor in developing the schedule is identifying the most critical processes. Some activities are more important than others or engender greater risk. These are usually audited more frequently. This criticality will vary from one organization to another. For example, an organization that refurbishes customer-owned machinery has a greater need to audit requirements for control of customer-owned property than one that only accepts parts from one customer for assembly into a job that's only done once or twice a year. Or, one organization may have a stable workforce with mature processes that require little new training, whereas another may have a dynamic mix of products that require training every few months. In the latter case, the training program may need to be audited with greater frequency. Another example would be customer data that is to be incorporated into a software product. In this case, the control of the customer property might fall under the organization's requirements for document control and would, therefore, be included in the assessment of document control practices. Because documentation is an essential element that permeates the entire QMS infrastructure, the criticality would indicate the need for more frequent audits. The control of customer data would automatically get assessed with comparable frequency. Conversely, there could be a process that was formerly riddled with problems that now has achieved an acceptable level of control, resulting in a diminished need for audits.

Frequency can also be affected by how the audits are structured. In some instances, fewer processes are audited during one audit, utilizing less time. The benefit is that auditors are away from their other jobs for shorter periods of time. This, however, results in the need for more frequent audits. In other cases, the organization opts for larger audits that encompass more processes and consume more time. These audits are more apt to reflect the process approach and produce better results. They also carry the advantage that they aren't usually done as frequently. The downside is that the auditors generally devote an entire day or more to each audit. There's no right way: Constraints have to be weighed against the benefits to be derived.

Other issues that affect decisions around frequency are the results of previous audits (including certification body, regulatory, and customer audits) or any other reports or corrective actions that suggest a heightened level of risk. For example, if a nonconformance was cited during the previous audit, there's already a need to return to verify that the corrective action taken has been effective. It's inappropriate to wait an entire year to see if the problem has been eliminated or ameliorated, so an increased frequency is advisable. Similarly, if there were several opportunities for improvement (OFIs) noted in the last audit, it might reflect a perception that control of processes is starting to erode or that documentation is not as clear as it could be. This might warrant reducing the time lapse between audits. If the process is usually only assessed once a year, it might be worth bumping it up to two audits annually until there is evidence to suggest that the level of risk has decreased.

It's important to note that the audit schedule should be reviewed periodically and revised as needed. Things change. Problems arise. New products get introduced. Volume increases. A second shift gets added. Key personnel leave or are re-assigned. A new ERP system gets installed. The ISO 9001 standard is revised. All of these factors affect your QMS. All of these mandate some level of response. One of the best ways to assess whether the response has been adequate to ensure that there's been no degradation in control is the internal audit process.

---

# Auditors

The first requirement is to ensure that auditors have adequate training. (More on this in chapter 3.) There's no excuse for sending out untrained or poorly trained auditors. The predictable results will be ineffective audits that waste company resources.

Once a pool of trained auditors has been established, there are a couple of decisions to make. One is the structure of the team. Will auditors be sent out individually or as teams—usually in pairs? Both models have their benefits: Teams ensure better coverage and increased objectivity; single auditors can sometimes work more quickly and efficiently.

Auditors may not audit their own work. Therefore, when developing the audit schedule and making the assignments, it's important to ensure that auditors, either individually or in teams, are independent of the processes they will be auditing. If an auditor works in the QC lab, he or she can't audit the inspection process. Or, if someone has recently been transferred from maintenance to the machine shop, that person may not audit the preventive maintenance processes because there's a high likelihood of auditing his or her own work.

## Prepping for each audit

The audit plan doesn't just materialize from thin air. Addressing the constraints and coordinating activities to make sure a thorough and balanced assessment occurs requires work. This is especially true when doing larger audits—or when conducting supplier audits or third-party assessments.

When I'm doing a surveillance audit, people seem to assume that auditors show up without any advance planning even when the organization has been sent the schedule in advance. They underestimate just how much up-front work goes into a good audit.

So what are some of the areas that have to be addressed? What questions would it be helpful to have answered before the audit schedule is put together? Here are a few issues you may want to consider:

- *Lunch (not yours).* If you're in a manufacturing facility that starts the day shift at 6:00 a.m., there's a good chance the production people will be taking lunch at 10:30 or 11:00 a.m. Also, it's important to know when they take their breaks. In some organizations, it doesn't matter if someone goes on break 15 minutes later than usual. However, in other facilities, breaks are timed to coincide with the arrival of the canteen truck. If they miss their break, they may also miss out on buying their lunches.

It's not uncommon for service departments to stagger lunch times to ensure coverage during the noon hour. However, that usually leaves phones understaffed, which in turn means the auditees are going to be distracted when trying to answer your questions. It's best to schedule their interviews when the staff is at full strength.

- *Deliveries.* If the UPS truck arrives at 9:30 a.m., you're not going to be able to observe the receipt of materials in the late afternoon. You may be able to assess inspection processes because that can happen at any time—usually after a sample has been transferred to the QC lab. In some environments this is no big deal. However, if the organization is accepting materials that require special handling or accompanying certifications, you want to be at the receiving dock when the deliveries come in.

- *Proximity.* If a facility is large or spread over several buildings, you may want to cluster processes so that you're not running back and forth between departments. Again, travel time is often identified as one of the "wastes" in lean projects. The concept applies here as well. Scurrying to and fro wastes precious time. Efficiency is as important to auditing as to other processes. For example, records may be kept in a different area—or building—from where a process is observed. To verify the status of calibrated tools, you may need to write down identification numbers and other pertinent data from calibration labels found on tools in several work centers that are being audited. You can check the records later when you get to the quality assurance area—or wherever the calibration records are maintained. The same may hold true for training records and other evidence of qualification. Because the auditor is gathering evidence from several process, this means that control of calibration and training processes should be scheduled later in the day or on a subsequent day for a multi-day audit.

# Documentation

Auditors need several documents and forms to conduct their audits. They should access and review the primary documents that describe the processes prior to the audit. And, unless the organization provides a pre-developed checklist, the auditor also needs time to develop questions based on the documents. Auditors are required to keep records of their findings. In some organizations, a specific controlled form is used for writing up nonconformities.

There are pros and cons to having internal auditors develop checklists. On the positive side, they are required to review the documents in order to generate the list of questions. This increases their preparedness for the interviews. It also keeps the audits fresh since auditors may use different questions to ascertain conformance to a requirement—or they may sequence their questions to follow a path to an ancillary process also being audited. This augments their understanding of the entire management system.

However, there are some benefits to the canned checklists as well. Important factors don't get missed—which can be a problem in regulatory environments. For newly trained auditors, checklists provide guidance until they develop their planning and interviewing skills. Checklists also help when there's a revision to a standard or if new requirements have been introduced into the QMS. In smaller organizations that struggle with time constraints, there may not be adequate time for auditors to create new checklists for each audit. Although this isn't a good excuse for using canned checklists, it's important to concede that sometimes it's the only option.

The downside to using canned checklists is that auditors are asking the exact same questions over and over again. The interviews become rote and auditors fall into the habit of checking things off as either yes or no. There's no following of audit trails or assessment of potential negative effects on other processes. The mechanical nature of the audit limits the opportunity for consideration that helps to make the audit meaningful. Chapter 4 provides guidance on developing audit checklists.

With sufficient training, a well-developed audit plan, and the necessary documentation in hand, auditors have a higher probability of conducting audits that are a benefit to the organization.

There are other factors that should be considered that don't apply to all organizations. The two most prominent ones are auditing multiple shifts and auditing field installations. Some organizations also have outsourced processes like remote storage, secondary material processing, or support activities carried out by sister divisions. The outsourced processes are often handled through the purchasing function and through supplier monitoring, which can at times include supplier audits. Second, third, or weekend shifts and off-site activities such as servicing and installations are QMS processes that should be included in the audit schedule. It's appropriate to spend a little time discussing why auditing these processes is important.

We've all heard the expression that an audit is a snapshot in time. Whatever is going on at a particular time should be representative of what occurs on any other typical day. The players are pretty much the same; the resources are fairly static. There's a better than even shot that whatever samplings of records and documents that the auditor reviews will be reflective of what would be seen on any other day. The underlying principle is that processes are well-controlled and are carried out uniformly because the environment in which they are occurring is stable and consistent.

The question that arises is, "Are processes on second and third shifts carried out with the same level of control?" Before responding, consider the fact that the environment on these shifts is often substantially different. Resources aren't as easily accessible; managers aren't a few offices away. Support staff, such as the people in IT or process engineers, have all gone home.

Many times, when a company has a second shift that starts at 3:00 p.m., the third-party auditor will seize the opportunity to interview these individuals during regular business hours. There's no questioning the efficiency of doing things when everyone is still around. But, unfortunately, you don't get to observe many of the "What if...?" kind of scenarios, because the resources and information are ready at hand and the managers are still at their desks. Many organizations have three shifts. Others may also have weekend hours. Restricting the audit to the traditional 8-to-5 business day deprives the organization of a complete and balanced audit program.

In the past several years, I've had two opportunities to include the second shift in surveillance audits. In both cases, I explained to the managers that it was important to assess the continued control of processes when office staff and managers were not available. Both managers were supremely confident that everything would play out just fine.

In one case, the processes did remain well-controlled. One manager remained on-site for several hours and was available by phone. A satellite location that was three time zones to the west could cover problems with late customer requests. Due to the need to support the other facility, the servers remained online. People had the necessary access to documents. Individuals received the same level of training as their daytime peers. There was little that couldn't be handled; what couldn't be handled could wait until the next day.

The other company I audited was a different matter. Individuals on the second shift had not received the same kind of refresher training on revised processes. Some of their documents were outdated. They often had to put jobs on hold because customer service representatives weren't around to answer their questions. Material wasn't located in the correct areas. The supervisory staff couldn't deal with many contingencies—the "What if...?" scenarios. The level of control was obviously inadequate for the type of work that was being done.

One of the things that I found interesting about both organizations is that it had never occurred to them to include the second shifts in their internal audits or to attempt to do an audit after the office staff had gone home.

It's important to consider the criticality of processes that are conducted during off hours. If the company is running a 24-7 production operation, there should be evidence that the support processes are in place or that adequate contingencies have been planned. With some companies, all that happens on these shifts are prep functions, preventive maintenance, or activities that require little supervision or support. However, in others, products and services are being produced and delivered around the clock. Inspection and tests are performed. Decisions are made. Material is shipped to customers.

Regardless of whether there's managerial staff on site during the off hours, it rarely occurs to the person managing the audit program to include a nighttime or weekend internal audit. Problems occurring on these shifts are often shrugged off as to be expected. They sometimes don't even get included in performance metrics.

There are two disadvantages to this omission. The first is that the organization has an incomplete picture of how it's doing. The output of the audit function is skewed. The other drawback is that it reinforces the subliminal message that people on the second shift aren't as important. This may be a factor in problems with morale that in turn contribute to the erosion of process control—"If no one cares, why should we?"

Auditing off-site processes such as field installation also allows observation of activities when support services are not readily at hand. Manuals and tools that are used solely by the installation crews may not get the same periodic assessment as materials at the plant. Process owners have to deal with work environment situations over which they have limited control. Things are not the same as in the controlled space at your facility. It's essential that these processes be included in the audit schedule. Unfortunately, this adds complexity to the overall audit plan. There are constraints that accompany both of these categories. Most trained internal auditors come from the day shift. This means plans have to be made for someone to stay late or come in early—or on the weekend. Because the frequency of these audits is reliant on criticality, it's important to assess the risk. If an organization that manufactures implantable medical devices is running 24-7, it's paramount that all shifts get audited at regular intervals. For off-site processes, there are time and travel constraints to factor in as well.

Now that we've looked at all the factors and constraints that must be considered as one puts together an audit program, we can take a look at what an annual audit schedule might look like. (This is different from the audit schedule that is put together for individual audits.)

There are two examples showing different frequencies. Each model has its benefits and drawbacks. In both cases, the entire QMS is audited over a twelve-month cycle. Some processes are audited more frequently than others. Both examples reflect the process approach in that inputs and outputs between processes, as well as ancillary factors, can be assessed, bringing much more value to the audit process. The other big challenge in both of these models is to ensure that all auditors are independent of the function. Actually, the strict rule is that auditors may not audit their own work. The easiest way to ensure independence is to have people who generally work in the office audit the manufacturing processes and vice versa. Other options sometimes available are people from different facilities, people working another shift, outside sales staff, or individuals from an unrelated department.

Table 1 shows audits being conducted every other month. Two teams of two auditors each are sent out to assess most of the features of

| Month | January | | March | | May | | July | |
|---|---|---|---|---|---|---|---|---|
| | Team 1 | Team 2 | Team 1 | Team 2 | Team 1 | Team 2 | Team 1 | Team 2 |
| Area | Production Line 1 | | Field Installation | | Software Development | | Production Line 2 | |
| | Purchasing | | Quoting | | Design | | Quoting | |
| | Receiving | | Order entry | | Engineering | | Order entry | |
| | | Production | | Installation | | Outsourced packaging | | Production |
| | | Inspection | | Inspection | | Testing | | Inspection |
| | | Shipping | Scheduling | Calibration | Training | | Scheduling | Calibration |
| | Warehousing & traceability | Lock-out/ tag-out | | Equipment maintenance | | Warehousing & traceability | | Equipment maintenance |
| | Control of N/C mat'l | | Control of N/C mat'l | | Control of N/C mat'l | | Control of N/C mat'l | |
| | Documentation | | Documentation | | Documentation | | Documentation | |
| | Records | | Records | | Records | | Records | |

Table 1, Part 1, Sample A: Annual Audit Program Schedule

| September | | November | December |
|---|---|---|---|
| Team 1 | Team 2 | Team 1 & Team 2 | Team 1 |
| Field Installation | | Production Line 1 & 2 (2nd shift) | QMS processes |
| Design | | | Internal audits |
| Engineering | | | Management review |
| | Installation | Production | Corrective actions |
| | Inspection | Inspection | Preventive actions |
| Training | | Shipping | Data analysis |
| | Lock-out/tag-out | Calibration | |
| Control of N/C mat'l | | Control of N/C mat'l | |
| Documentation | | Documentation | Documentation |
| Records | | Records | Records |

Table 1, Part 2, Sample A: Annual Audit Program Schedule

a defined area. This organization has four unique product units: Production Line 1, Production Line 2, Software Development, and Field Installation. Although each area of the production lines only gets audited once per year, there is such a significant amount of overlap that the processes and requirements will get audited several times per year. The quoting and order processing (normally referred to as "contract review") is done once for the production line (which will inevitably include the accompanying software package) and once for a field installation. Document control, records maintenance, and control of nonconforming material show up during each audit. These three processes are systemic and pervade the entire system.

Because the audits are less frequent and more auditors are assigned, each audit (conducted in alternate months) is much more in-depth. It will require both teams about two days to complete the audits. However, depending on the size of the auditor pool the organization has, they may only be called upon to do audits twice a year.

Table 2 varies in that audits are conducted every month. (Only part of the audit schedule is shown in this illustration.) One team of two auditors goes out and covers all elements scheduled. The team is smaller, and because the audits are more frequent, the checklists may be shorter. These

| Area | Production Line 1 | | Field Installation | | Software Development | |
|---|---|---|---|---|---|---|
| Month | January | October | February | July | March | September |
| | Team 1 | Team 2 | Team 1 | Team 2 | Team 1 | Team 2 |
| **Processes/requirements** | Purchasing | | Quoting | | Design | |
| | Receiving | | Order entry | | Engineering | |
| | Production | | Installation | | Outsourced packaging | |
| | Inspection | | Inspection | | Testing | |
| | Shipping | | Scheduling | | Training | |
| | Lock-out/tag-out | | Equipment maintenance | | Warehousing & traceability | |
| | Control of N/C mat'l | | Control of N/C mat'l | | Control of N/C mat'l | |
| | Training | | Calibration | | Documentation | |
| | Documentation | | Documentation | | Records | |
| | Records | | Records | | | |

Table 2, Sample B: Annual Audit Program Schedule

audits may take up to one day. Again, the size of the audit pool will determine how frequently auditors are asked to conduct audits. The benefit of this model is that each area gets visited by an audit team twice per year.

There are many variations on the two models presented. It's important to remember to make sure that there is adequate auditing of the most critical functions, that the audits reflect the process approach, that auditors must be independent of the work being audited, and that over the course of a defined period (usually one year) everything gets seen at least once.

Plans only have worth if they are used. Putting all this effort into planning the program, developing a schedule, and creating checklists is a futile endeavor if the organization is going to continually find excuses to delay audits—with the oft-cited excuse that the auditors are too busy with their "real" jobs. Similarly, it makes no sense to put together a plan that makes it impossible for auditors to utilize good audit practices, such as the process approach or following audit trails. The audits lack the holistic perspective that allows auditors to determine effectiveness or to observe problems and risks that span multiple activities. Both of these attitudes endanger the entire audit program because they create the impression that audits aren't important—that audits have no value.

These are the major factors that go into planning an efficient audit. When initially setting up an audit program, make sure to include adequate time for thoughtful planning. Like so many other things, this small investment can pay big dividends. Develop good plans and use them!

# CHAPTER 2

# Drive Fear Out of the Audit Process

I t was the great W. Edwards Deming who first applied this tenet, "Drive out fear," to quality management in his book *Out of the Crisis* (Massachusetts Institute of Technology, 1982). It's one of his 14 Points for Management. Fear-driven systems cripple an organization's ability to innovate, respond to change, deal with risk, and manage problems. People who are afraid of failure, retribution, punitive action, and job loss are reluctant to offer suggestions, try new techniques, speak up about risks, or admit errors. A company that fosters a culture of fear disables its employees' ability to contribute to the long-term sustainable success of the business.

Let's look at how fear drives some of the negative baggage surrounding auditing and how vanquishing this fear will allow us to experience more genuine benefit from this much-maligned process.

We can start by examining the textbook definition of "audit" found in ISO 19011: "…systematic, independent, and documented process for obtaining audit evidence and evaluating it objectively to determine the extent to which audit criteria are fulfilled." No mention of consequences for evil-doers and no suggestion of punitive action, not even a passing mention of findings of nonconformance. Auditing is about evaluating a system against defined criteria. What happens after the audit is up to us.

Now let's consider the players: There are the auditees, the client (usually the management group of the organization), and the auditors. The auditees are the people who respond to the auditors questions. These individuals are afraid of auditors. It doesn't matter if it's a first-, second-, or third-party audit. Auditees don't want to be the cause of a nonconformance. They don't want to get dinged. They will go to great lengths to avoid the dreaded nonconformance. They will try to cast situations in the most favorable light; they'll conceal problems; they might even lie. Because despite the fact that we say that it's about finding opportunities to improve, our tone and our manner often suggest otherwise.

How far-reaching can the consequences of this kind of culture be? Several years ago, one of my clients went through an ISO 9001 implementation and certification process. During the course of the audit, one minor nonconformance was cited. The individual who had responsibility for the area where the nonconformance was discovered was devastated. In his mind, he was being blamed for the only mar on an otherwise perfect audit. He perceived the corrective action request that he was given as his punishment for having caused the nonconformance.

To alleviate his distress I explained to him that he had received the request because he was the person best qualified to address the problem and help fix it. The company was asking him for his assistance. To this he replied, "All right, then I will tell you the truth." Up until that moment he was afraid of the consequences if it was learned that he'd modified machine settings—with the very laudable goal of increasing throughput, thereby increasing efficiency. He hadn't considered the effect on the next process and he hadn't told anyone what he had done. But, he'd had a very good idea.

Without encouragement, three things would have happened:
- The problem would have persisted.
- We would've never gotten to the root cause because he would have done everything he could to conceal his culpability out of fear of losing his job.
- He would have stopped thinking of ways to improve his process.

It's not just about morale or having a feel-good environment in which to work. It's directly relevant to an organization's ability to investigate problems thoroughly, to uncover the information that will allow it to improve, and to elicit innovative ideas from its workforce.

Of course, this is just a reflection of the fear that's been impressed upon them by top management. Look at their attitude toward certification bodies (also known as registrars). I've observed audits where the auditor was wrong; and I told my client that he should challenge the finding. "Oh, no. We don't want to upset the auditor. We don't want to get dinged with any majors or minors." This fear is communicated down to the rest of the organization.

This takes us to the second group of terrified players in the audit process: the managers.

We've all heard the expression from managers and supervisors about their desire for a "clean" audit. It usually refers to a registrar's surveillance audit or some other third-party assessment, but it's often applied to internal audits as well. A few days prior to the visit, managers gather the troops, give a pre-game pep talk, and end with a rousing exhortation to have a clean audit.

There's little time spent telling people to be honest with the auditors. We don't hear: "Don't worry about this. Audits help us find problems that need to be fixed and opportunities to improve. Whatever the auditors find should help us to get better." To the contrary, I've seen organizations who have set a quality objective of "zero audit findings." There's no such thing as a consistently perfect organization. If there are no audit findings over the course of several audits, the auditors aren't doing their jobs and/or the auditees are hiding things.

Richard Bach wrote: "There is no such thing as a problem without a gift for you in its hands. You seek problems because you need their gifts." How interesting it would be if we accepted audit findings in the same spirit. But this can't happen if we hide things to ensure we have a "clean audit."

If there are clean audits, is it also possible to have "dirty audits"? And, if so, what would characterize such audits? Would the auditors make a mess of the calibration area? Would there be disorganized files strewn across the sales manager's desk? Would the production floor be awash in blood? Would the audit report be peppered with slanderous accusations, profane language, and naughty illustrations? Or, even more horrible, would the audit report include the dreaded and vile nonconformity?

Based on the reaction a nonconformity generally generates, you'd almost expect a dictionary definition to read something like this: "An event of putrefying and soul-sucking proportion, purported to end careers and cause ISO 9001 certificates to spontaneously combust."

What is it with people and nonconformances? Bosses look upon them as a personal indictment of their managerial competence, the president of the company views them as some kind of barometer of organizational stability, and individuals perceive them as the report card from hell that will get them fired. Nonconformances are just observations that things aren't being done the way they should be and that there's a risk to the organization if there's no action taken to change the situation.

Let's recap just what it means to receive an audit report that includes a finding of nonconformity—even a major nonconformity.

The auditor has identified that there has been the "nonfulfillment of a requirement." That's the definition of a nonconformity as found in ISO 9000:2005 Quality management systems—Fundamentals and vocabulary. Either a product was not made in conformance to specifications or some other requirement has not been met. For example, it may be that a procedure states that appointments for auto glass replacement must be confirmed between 8:00 a.m. and 8:30 a.m. on the day of the technician's visit. The auditor observed that the customer service representative was doing the confirmation calls in the late afternoon on the day prior to the appointment. There's obviously a nonconformance. However, it may be that the company figured out that confirming the appointment the day before made a lot more sense and modified the process without revising the documented procedure.

The genuine concern here, and the real reason that this should be addressed, is that the organization must ensure that individuals aren't changing processes without revising the corresponding documentation.

It's a bad habit that can lead to a proliferation of uncontrolled documents and processes. Eventually, no one knows what the right thing is supposed to be and mistakes are inevitable—some with more dire consequences than a missed appointment.

Errors and degradations in process control evolve over time. They mostly result from change. Individuals retire, get promoted, or leave. Their replacements aren't as knowledgeable in the details of the process and the older documentation isn't very helpful. Customers' requirements change. What used to be acceptable is now rejected because they've tightened up dimensional tolerances or some other product attributes. New equipment is purchased that eliminates the need for tedious steps that had been laboriously described in wordy work instructions that never got updated. Tooling wears. Then, there are the actual cases where someone simply failed to do the right thing. There was an operator error.

In so many instances things change and we're just not paying attention. So, isn't it a great idea to have audits that catch process nonconformities before they result in product defects? Isn't it more advantageous to address problems before they become catastrophes?

Upon being "dinged"—another questionable expression that has crept into our quality management system (QMS) lexicon—with a nonconformity, we proceed to investigate the root cause and figure out how to address it. We revise the process, fix the documents, do some training, and end up with an improved practice and a more enlightened workforce. Overall, not a bad outcome from a process steeped in fear and loathing— a process that is supposed to be objective, nonconfrontational, and intended to drive improvement.

The final players in this process are the auditors. They fear alienation from co-workers, aggravation from the boss who wanted a "clean audit," and, in the case of third-party assessments, the fear that too many findings will result in an unhappy registrar who, in turn, fears losing a paying client to a more lenient certification body.

The certification bodies are afraid of losing clients; organizations are afraid of getting nonconformances; bosses are afraid of poor performance ratings; auditors are afraid of getting fired; and the person on the manufacturing floor just wants to run for cover. This is almost laughable.

The result of a fear-laden audit process is that we end up devaluing a key component of our organization's QMS. Internal audits provide the information that drives the improvements that perpetuate an organization's ability to continue to serve its customers. Supplier audits strengthen the supply chain. For third-party audits (such as an ISO 9001 certification audit), the audits provide objective assessments that increase customers' confidence in the suppliers' ability to meet their needs. Fear actually imperils the integrity of the conformity assessment industry. This is unfortunate because in this global economy that loss of integrity reflects poorly on the organizations that have implemented and are maintaining an internationally recognized effective QMS. A robust audit program is a very desirable thing.

The other factor that feeds the fear permeating the audit process is our attitude toward evidence—the fodder of detective stories, the bane of criminals, the undoing of fiends. From Sherlock Holmes to Perry Mason, evidence lights the fuse for the climactic "Aha!" that illuminates the denouement where all is finally revealed. The current offering of criminal investigation shows perpetuate the image of dogged investigators chasing down the clues that will lead to the eventual arrest of the villain.

Evidence is the stuff in whodunits that proves the bad guy did it. In our judicial system the burden of proof is on the prosecution. Evidence is more commonly associated with indictment of the guilty party rather than exoneration of the innocent, despite the obvious fact that it can be used to substantiate either. Is it any wonder that auditees ascribe such a negative connotation to the whole concept of evidence gathering? Or that they cringe at the mere arrival of the dreaded auditor? It's not very often you'll hear an individual say, "I'm dying for the auditor to show up so I can show her all the cool things we're doing."

Joe Friday, the poker-faced gumshoe from "Dragnet," was probably the only character who got it right: "Just the facts, ma'am." In that one simple sentence he conveyed the essence of evidence gathering. It's about assembling a selection of facts—generally found in records—in order to find out about something. In the case of an audit, it's to find out if the defined requirements have been met.

Auditors bandy the term "evidence" about a lot. They need evidence to substantiate their conclusion as to the organization's conformance to requirements. Unfortunately, when auditors are asked why they need the evidence, their demeanor supports the auditees' impressions that the auditors are looking to see if the auditees are screwing up. Auditors are perceived as being in fault-finding mode instead of fact-finding mode.

Too many auditors have a "Aha! Gotcha!" attitude when they find a nonconformance. It's important to remain objective and unperturbed. The conversation with the auditee should basically convey, "This is the documented requirement and this is the record; they don't match." No accusatory tone; no suggestion of wrongdoing. The input and the output don't match. Period.

Auditors don't do a particularly stellar job of pointing out all the bits of evidence that are harbingers of good news. Audit reports are skewed toward the findings of nonconformity and the opportunities for improvement (which are really articulations of perceived risk that should be addressed before something does go wrong). Auditors don't spend nearly as much ink—or bytes—on the positive stuff. They aren't as diligent in mentioning the processes that have improved since the last audit, the goals that have been achieved, the decrease in errors, the success stories coming out of a well-implemented corrective action. What the auditee hears in the closing meeting is a litany of everything bad, with only the sparsest of nods to any positive observations. Even if the audit report does convey laudatory comments for improvements and innovations, the kind words rarely reach the individuals who trembled through their audit interviews.

Auditors begin with the somewhat adversarial premise that until something is proven to be compliant, there is no justification to presume that it is indeed compliant. That's the "show me" approach. The opposite tactic would have the auditor presuming that everything is great until evidence is presented to the contrary. That approach carries its own risk.

Auditors make reasonable conclusions based upon assessment of an adequate sampling of evidence. Failing to find fault does not necessarily mean that everything is perfect.

And, lack of evidence is not always indicative of noncompliance. In a recent "Nova" episode on PBS, a physicist was talking about a new and as yet unproven hypothesis about the nature and origin of our universe. He said, "You can choose to believe whatever you wish, because we haven't yet been able to prove these things." Sometimes there just isn't any evidence available at the time of the audit. If the company has a robust process for controlling customer-owned property, but there doesn't happen to be any in the plant on the day of the audit, it doesn't mean that—in the absence of evidence—the process is uncontrolled. Documentation presented and anecdotal evidence of what would happen if there were customer property to be handled is all that the auditor has to go on. Without further proof, the only conclusion based on what's available is that the established process provides adequate control to handle the contingency.

Which brings us back to Joe Friday. Auditors should begin with a clean slate—no presumptions. "Just the facts." And, then see where the trail of evidence leads.

Auditors probably can't completely alleviate auditee fears when they hear the word "evidence," but auditors should try to communicate the fact that evidence, in and of itself, is neither positive nor negative. Until it is assessed against requirements and in consideration of application, a piece of evidence is just a factoid. It's simply a vehicle to get us where we need to go—an objective and meaningful audit report. And, it's definitely not about finding the bad guy.

What can we do to dispel fear around auditing?

- Management must communicate that audits are welcome opportunities to improve the organization.
- The organization needs to stop using zero findings as a meaningful quality objective.
- Management must ensure that no punitive action is taken for audit findings.

- Auditees must be encouraged to be truthful, open, and thorough with auditors.
- Auditors need to subdue the negative body language and tone around evidence and findings of nonconformance.
- Everybody needs to relax.

CHAPTER 3

# Ensure Adequate Training

Regardless of whether an auditor is conducting an internal or an external audit, there's no excuse for ignoring good audit practices.

I often get asked about the amount of training internal auditors need. Actually, the question is more like: "What is the absolute, ABSOLUTE, least amount of training we can get away with and still have auditors who'll be considered 'qualified' by our ISO auditor?"

First of all, the person asking isn't reflecting on the fact that they've addressed the question to an auditor. That's kind of like asking a physician the least amount of courses you need to claim you're a qualified surgeon—or tantamount to complaining to a master electrician that anything more than one week of apprenticeship is absurd overkill and outrageously unnecessary. The individual has basically just intimated his or her disdain for the auditing process and for the auditing profession. Frankly, the question is, at best, disrespectful.

Of even greater concern, is what the question bodes in terms of the success and effectiveness of the organization's internal auditing program. Considering the fact that the question usually comes from senior managers, it's clear that that their opinion of internal audits reflects their failure to perceive any value. That's unfortunate and shortsighted. I want to ask them: "If you consider auditing to be so worthless, why bother at all? Save your money. But, also, forget about being ISO-compliant, because you won't be. ...Or, you will be, but only for a short period of time because your system will fall apart."

A colleague once commented that internal auditors will not be fully valued and respected until such time as they are accorded the same regard as financial auditors. Despite the fact that internal auditors do for the organization's management system processes what financial auditors do for their accounting processes, there is enormous disparity in how the two professions are perceived.

Consider this: If you don't manage your processes well and periodically assess how well they are managed, there will be fewer beans for the bean counters to count and proportionally fewer records for the CPAs to audit.

We expect financial auditors to be trained. In fact, we expect them to be well-educated. If we found out that their credentials came from some two-bit diploma mill, we'd fire them. We expect thorough and reliable financial audit results. Why then do we not hold at least a modicum of the same expectations for our internal auditors?

Internal auditors who are well trained and have been afforded the time and resources to conduct thorough audits provide their top management with a wealth of information about the status of the organization. They can objectively report what's working well, what risks have been perceived, and what problems need to be addressed. They present management an unbiased and balanced assessment of how things are running. This can be used to make decisions relative to strategic plans, allocation of resources, and prioritization of projects.

There's significant responsibility inherent in the audit profession. Good auditors take seriously their charge to make an objective assessment of the organization. Their reports reflect deliberation and thoughtfulness that can only come with good training and practice.

It's just like any other aspect of an enterprise. The willingness to invest in this organizational asset should pay dividends. You can't reap those rewards if you're trying to do things on the cheap.

Training should result in the following abilities:

- Comprehension of auditor traits, role, code of conduct, and confidentiality

- Understanding of documented requirements
- Planning
- Time management
- Development of audit checklists
- Comprehension of the process approach and interrelation of processes
- Communication skills
- Interviewing skills
- Assessment of records, inspection reports, statistical data
- Understanding of the nature of nonconformances
- Writing audit reports
- Following-up on corrective actions

Additionally, as appropriate to the industry, there may be a need for training in regulatory compliance issues, safety protocols, and specific record-retention practices.

What kind of training is appropriate? Auditors should have formal instruction in audit fundamentals, audit techniques, audit planning, and report writing. The instruction should be offered by an individual or organization who has the expertise and skills to ensure the learning process is effective. It's important to select an individual or outside provider who can teach your auditors to conduct effective assessments.

Occasionally there is someone internal to the organization who can do the training. There's a common assumption that quality managers should be adept at auditor training. Although some quality managers may understand the quality management system (QMS), regulatory standards, and customer requirements, they may not have the requisite skill set to teach others how to audit. In some cases, they may not even be auditors themselves.

I once had occasion to audit an organization that had individuals shadow an internal auditor for one or two audits. Afterward, they were deemed qualified to conduct audits on their own. They received no instruction in audit preparation, interviewing, objective evidence, or report writing. This kind of practice only perpetuates the disregard for the audit process.

For supplier audits, use of untrained auditors is not only a waste of your organization's time, but it also wastes the supplier's time. Any organization that undergoes an audit has the right to expect to reap some benefit from the audit in the form of identifications of risk, opportunities for improvement, or even corrective action requests. That's impossible if the individual who presumes to conduct the audit has no idea of how to objectively assess the system.

In most cases, it's worth the investment to get auditors trained by an outside source. In all instances, their ability to meet the learning objectives listed earlier should be the main criteria for selection. There are a lot of options from which to choose. Here are a few to consider:

- *A training program that leads to auditor Certified Quality Auditor (CQA) certification from the American Society for Quality provides auditors with a broad and strong foundation in the entire auditor body of knowledge.* It goes beyond simply filling out forms and asking questions. Individuals trained in one of these programs are exposed to methods and techniques that augment their ability to deliberate objectively and arrive at justifiable audit conclusions. Costs associated with this kind of training may be a bit high, but the payback is considerable. There's a lot of benefit in this training even if individuals ultimately don't sit for the exam. CQAs make good auditors.

- *Training offered by consultants and training organizations have varying degrees of rigor in their programs.* It's important to research qualifications to make sure they're providing what you need. The list of learning objective mentioned earlier is a good guide. Auditors should be able to demonstrate competence and knowledge by the end of the training program. Costs vary greatly. Organizations should be able to find one in their price range.

- *Lead assessor programs targeting a specific international standard—such as ISO 9001.* These programs have the benefit of teaching individuals about assessing requirements to a defined standard. They provide a lot of insight into the particular management system model that may help auditors understand systems. But, because the focus is on the standard, there isn't enough time devoted to audit technique. Auditors learn what to look for but not how to look for it. These programs are often pricey without providing enough of the audit fundamentals. Although they are essential for most lead assessor certifications, they aren't the best choice for training internal auditors.

- *The in-house trainers should be exactly that: trainers.* They should have demonstrated training ability and have adequate expertise in the subject matter. "On-the-job" training is not appropriate for internal auditors. If your organization has one or more individuals with the requisite training expertise, that's a great asset! This is a resource that should be utilized fully. These experienced auditors may serve as mentors. They don't do the original training but provide support and guidance as new auditors conduct their initial audits and write their first reports.

Beyond the need to have competent individuals conducting audits there are other benefits to be derived from having a well-trained team. The skills developed as auditors are transferable to other activities. Because of the analytical nature of auditing, the ability to amass evidence, and to perceive patterns, auditors make good problem solvers. They can bring these skills to the root cause analysis process, helping others to understand the dependencies and connections between seemingly disparate factors. Through a systemic approach honed through a better understanding of the interrelation of processes they can make meaningful contributions in the development of effective corrective action plans.

Finally, internal auditors are better prepared to respond to external auditors—from regulatory agencies, certification bodies, or customers. They understand requirements and what kind of evidence provides evidence of fulfillment. It adds value to the audit experience by augmenting the learning and the chance to uncover opportunities to improve.

Invest in your auditors' training and development and grant them the respect they deserve. Given half a chance, they'll repay your confidence and trust by proving themselves to be a great asset to your organization.

# CHAPTER 4

# Create Effective Checklists

The purpose of checklists is to guide the audit. They provide prompts of important requirements that must be verified and ensure that factors don't get forgotten or excluded. They facilitate the flow of the interview and contribute to effective time management.

Without good checklists audits can quickly fragment into a disjointed series of conversations with no clear intent. It's difficult to derive salient information and to follow audit trails when there's no logical assessment of process inputs, documented requirements, and evidence of results—not to mention ancillary factors such as training, work environment, tools, and other resources.

I discourage the use of checklists that result in only "yes" or "no" responses because they often result in long lists of "Ys" and "Ns." There's no mention of the job that was being worked on, what field service was being performed (or when or where), or what training records were reviewed. There is no evidence to substantiate the audit conclusion that the process is well controlled. Additionally, there's no reflection of the process approach or the assessment of control of interdependencies, communication, or effectiveness. This is less than half a job. Because they create little value, except in those instances when an auditor finally gets a "no" answer and writes up a corrective action request, the internal audit degenerates into a mundane chore that carries no appreciable benefit or significance to anyone.

## Activities

- Requesting quotations
- Supplier qualification
- Auditing
- Self-assessments
- Verify certifications
- Purchase materials
- Review specifications
- Check delivery
- Verify other QA requirements
- Receive product
- Inspect/accept
- Record traceability (if needed)
- Monitor/analyze data

Requirements

Ensure purchased product conforms to requirements

Qualify/select suppliers

Buy material; purchase services

Receive/inspect/ accept product

Monitor/suppliers; take action

Are outputs effective?

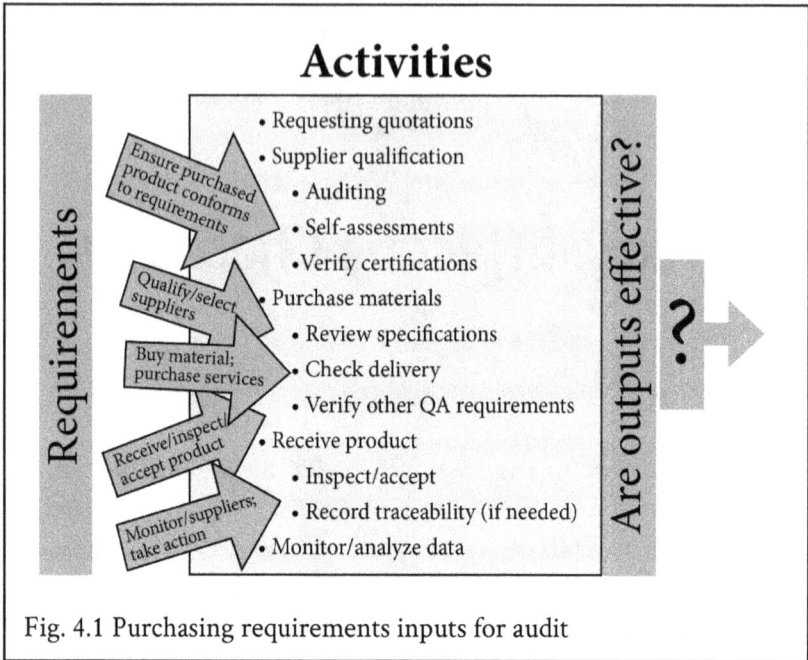

Fig. 4.1 Purchasing requirements inputs for audit

Audit checklists should be developed with an understanding of the processes to be audited. They should be prepared based upon review of defined requirements. If, for example, the scope of an audit is the purchasing and receiving processes, it will be necessary to review requirements in multiple procedures and work instructions to be able to put together a checklist that follows the flow of the inputs and outputs through the two distinct processes. It may also be necessary to check documents relating to control of nonconforming product (if the received material is not acceptable), inspection procedures (if receiving includes incoming inspection), and the calibration list (if the inspection requires calibrated equipment). Note that the entire calibration process is not going to be audited.

This leads to the next point in developing the checklist. It's important to stay within the scope of the audit. But, at the same time, it's essential to assess support processes—as they relate to what is being audited. For the calibration list example mentioned above, it would be adequate to observe if the instruments are identified and have a sticker denoting their calibration status. For defective material, it would be appropriate to ensure that individuals know how to handle the material and to verify that it is properly controlled. The review, dispositioning, etc. would be beyond the scope of the audit.

Let's look at the overall requirements for the purchasing and receiving processes and see what questions would determine if the processes are controlled in accordance with documented requirements and if they are effective in fulfilling the intent. Figure 4.1 shows the requirements for purchasing and receiving.

To develop a checklist for these two processes (purchasing and receiving), the auditor will want to ask questions relative to the following:

- *Purchasing requirements.* What needs to be purchased, including possible requirements for material traceability, third-party testing, use of specifically trained/licensed personnel, etc.? Note that the input to this process may be embedded in the MRP program, tied to a customer contract, or found in purchase requisitions.
- *Qualification of suppliers.* This includes criteria for qualification, method of selection, records of assessment or third-party QMS certification, capacity, and capability to fulfill requirements. Because this might also include qualification of providers of outsourced services, there might be a need for additional assessment of controls, as appropriate to the criticality of the process.
- *Purchasing documents.* These include purchase orders (accuracy and adequacy of information relating to product and delivery), addenda (such as drawings or specifications), the method of communicating the order to the supplier, and the probable receipt of an acknowledgment.
- *Receiving materials.* These include the process for receiving; acceptance criteria; inspection and test (including sampling plan), if required; and communication of status of accepted material, including records of any required traceability such as lot codes or serial numbers.
- *Monitoring of supplier performance.* This includes established criteria for monitoring (quality, delivery, receipt of certificates or other documentation, etc.), method of analyzing and reporting performance, and any

actions taken, such as corrective actions or removal from approved supplier list.

So, the flow of the audit might look like figure 4.2.

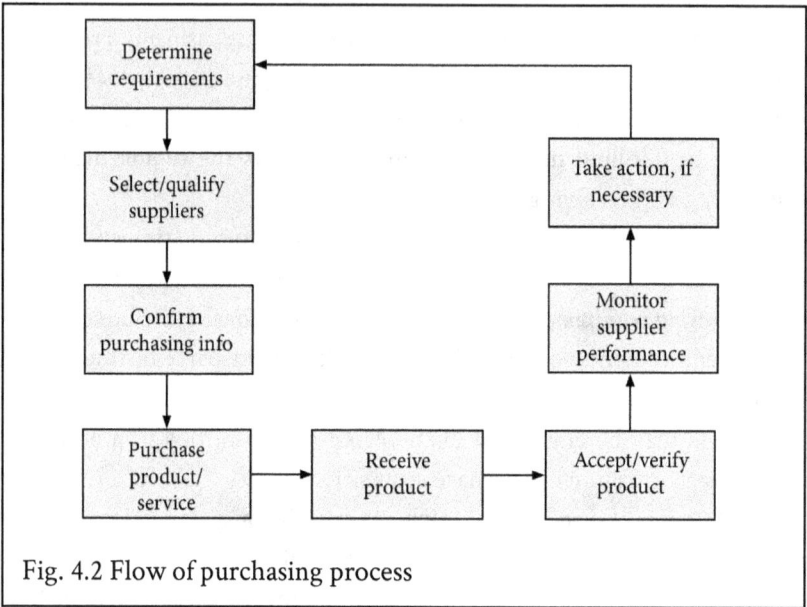

Fig. 4.2 Flow of purchasing process

The checklist for this audit would include questions about each of the steps in the process as defined in documented procedures. At the end of the audit, the auditor will be able to conclude that the process is both well controlled and effective if the material received is what is required and if it arrives on time with any mandated documentation.

Figure 4.3 demonstrates a typical checklist.

The checklist should have room for comments and for reporting the evidence observed. If an audit was being conducted in the engineering area, the following questions would be appropriate: What design project is being worked on? Are there test results embedded in the first review?

Was there a list of deliverables or actions items that came out of the design review? To whom were they assigned? Answers to these questions must be recorded. Writing things down proves that there is justifiable

| Requirement | Document or Procedure # ISO requirement | Comments/records/evidence | OK N/C OFI |
|---|---|---|---|
| How are suppliers qualified? Where are the records of approval? | SOP-463-01 ISO 7.4.1 | | |
| Is the process different for out-sourced processes? | WI-463-01-01 ISO 4.1 | | |
| What information is required on the purchase orders? Any document accompany order? | SOP-463-01 ISO 7.4.2 | | |
| What is required when the material is received? For inspection, describe the sampling plan used. | SOP-450-01 ISO 7.4.3 | | |
| How are the suppliers monitored? | SOP-463-01 ISO 8.4 (d) | | |
| Resource and support requirements | | | |
| Control of revision level of documents sent to suppliers. | SOP-433-02 ISO 4.2.3 | | |
| Control of nonconforming material from suppliers | SOP-450-01 SOP-422-02 ISO 8.3 | | |
| Calibration of equipment used for incoming inspection | SOP-443-02 ISO 7.6 | | |

Fig. 4.3 Sample checklist for purchasing process

objective evidence for the audit conclusion. And, recording the information also demonstrates that the process was well enough controlled that the auditor was able to follow it.

The checklist in figure 4.3 has been compressed to fit on to one page in this book. However, when developing a checklist it's advisable to allow adequate space in the right column for recording responses and evidence assessed. This checklist when printed should be expanded to at least two pages to allow enough room to write things down. For the purposes of this example, the information in the column would include the names of three or four suppliers, the evidence used to qualify them, purchase orders placed with the qualified suppliers, records of receipt of materials, evidence of inspection or material acceptance, records of supplier monitoring (e.g., quarterly analysis), and records of any actions, including corrective actions.

| Job number | 7.1 |
|---|---|
| Raw material lot number | 7.5.3 |
| Record material lot number | 7.5.1 |
| Record of kitting | 7.5.1 |
| Sign off for multiple tasks (x 5) | 8.2.4 |
| Verification of inspections (x 3) | 7.6 |
| Inspection devices used | 7.6 |
| Serial numbers | 7.5.3 |
| Handling practices | 7.5.5 |
| Customer-supplied packaging | 7.5.4 |

Fig. 4.4 ISO 9001 requirements audited in production area

The example shown in figure 4.4 illustrates organizing the checklist for a manufacturing process. In this case the auditor could choose to use the job traveler (also called work order, router, ticket, etc.) to follow the process from planning to packaging. The intent is to verify effective fulfillment of requirements and conformance to the various clauses of ISO 9001.

The checklist in figure 4.5 will follow this process flow, with additional questions for support processes, such as calibration, training, and document control. Like the previous checklist, it has been compressed to one page. Because this audit could cover operations at multiple stations, it's quite likely that it would be three or four pages long.

There are additional questions that could be asked. They could relate to equipment maintenance, training, rework, or statistical methods—such as SPC—employed. This allows me to make another point: Questions can change with each audit. During one audit, a decision may be made to spend more time looking at everyone's training records. During a subsequent audit, the focus may shift to control of documentation packages. If there are multiple operations, the manager of the audit program may direct the auditors to look at only half of the operations during one audit and conduct a separate audit later on in the annual cycle to assess the rest.

| Requirement | Document or Procedure # ISO requirement | Comments/records/evidence | OK N/C OFI |
|---|---|---|---|
| Describe how routings are established for jobs and how jobs are scheduled | SOP-471-01 ISO 7.5.1 | | |
| Explain the kitting process | WI-472-01-01 ISO 4.1 | | |
| Describe _____ process | WI-472-01-01 WI-476-01-02 WI-478-01-02 ISO 7.5.1 | | |
| What type of inspection/ test is done? | SOP-454-01 ISO 8.2.4 | | |
| Describe any special handling requirements? How do you handle customer property? | SOP-478-01 ISO 7.5.5 ISO 7.5.4 | | |
| **Resource and support requirements** | | | |
| Control of revision level of documents included in production traveler packet | SOP-433-02 ISO 4.2.3 | | |
| Control of nonconforming material from in-process defects – or defective ma- terials | SOP-450-01 SOP-422-02 ISO 8.3 | | |
| Calibration of equipment used for in-process and final inspection | SOP-443-02 ISO 7.6 | | |
| How do you maintain traceability of materials being used? | SOP-478-03 ISO 7.5.3 | | |

Fig. 4.5 Sample checklist for manufacturing processes

The other item that can be added to the checklist might relate to veri-fication of corrective actions that have been implemented. This is an effi-cient and effective practice for closing out corrective actions. It's efficient in that by having the auditors verify the corrective actions, a separate au-dit or verification doesn't have to be scheduled. It's an effective practice in that the auditor can observe how well the corrective action is working within the process—and not as a unique anomaly.

Organizations can use basic templates to abbreviate the time it takes to create the audit checklist. In a regulated industry there might be several questions that must be asked during the course of every audit. For example, complete and signed-off device history records are critical to the medical device industry. A checklist can be set up with these mandatory questions, but the bulk of the audit checklist should be created by the internal auditors. It prepares them for the audit and improves their efficiency and time management.

With the use of a well-prepared checklist, the audit should flow easily. There's a greater chance of "quality" audit results. And, when it's complete, the responses on the checklist provided all the information needed to generate a meaningful audit report.

# CHAPTER 5

# Hone Your Interviewing Skills

A sking questions would seem to be a fairly straightforward activity. You ask a question; you get an answer. However, not everyone has the same comfort level when it comes to asking specific questions or when the context is a focused process rather than a casual conversation.

Interviewing skills should be developed and honed over time. The purpose of an audit interview is to gather objective information to determine the level of control of a given process. Are requirements understood? Does the process owner have the requisite competence and/or training? Are tools, documents, and other resources available? Is the output of the process what is intended? Do all these things conform to the requirements of the standard being used for the audit? Is everything working the way it's supposed to?

At the end of the interview, the auditor should have adequate evidence to conclude whether the process conforms to requirements and if it is effective. The following tips are useful in achieving the audit interview's goals:

- *Remember that auditees weren't hired to answer your questions.* They're paid to do their jobs. They're nervous and unaccustomed to being interviewed—even by a co-worker. They probably won't be quoting text verbatim from a procedure. Process owners should be describing their process in a way that lets you understand it and that demonstrates how well they understand it. Having them clearly articulate their responsibilities, the documents they use, and the steps in their process is the best indicator of their competence and awareness to perform the task. This, in turn, is a great indicator of how well controlled and effective the process is.

- *Ask open-ended questions, as opposed to the kind that will get only yes or no responses.* An interview that requires the auditee to explain will result in more complete and thoughtful responses. The yes/no question is like taking a true or false quiz. They have a 50 percent chance of giving you the answer you want. And, your notes will be sparse, lacking the details that justify any creditable audit conclusion.

- *Give the auditee an opportunity to explain what he or she does.* The person will provide more complete information if he or she isn't being steered toward the auditor's preconceived notion of what the answer should be.

- *Ask how the auditee does his or her job.* You're not just trying to verify that something is done; you want to verify that it's done correctly—as defined. Sometimes there are multiple methods to accomplish a task, but not all are correct and some may result in problems further down the line. In some cases, the sequence of steps must be followed exactly or the resulting product will not be acceptable—a fact that may not be immediately apparent. There are also those instances where the methods are defined by regulatory requirements.

- *Remember to use documents to help you frame your questions.* In chapter one the need to review documents prior to the audit was discussed. This lets you determine if the documentation accurately reflects the requirements of the process.

- *Listen to the auditee.* Practice your listening skills. Are you hearing what the person is saying or what you anticipate his or her answer to be? Because we've read the requirements before beginning the audit, we have a preconceived notion of what the response should be. Just because someone says something that surprises you or is inconsistent with a procedure doesn't mean that he or she is wrong. Hear the person out—with an objective ear. Listening is facilitated by the simple practice of looking directly at the person who's speaking. Not only do you remain better focused, you convey to the other person that you're interested in what he or she has to say.

- *Use the "show me" tactic.* This is especially useful if you aren't understanding what the auditee is trying to describe. Ask him or her to perform a task, to record the results of a test, or to find a customer's contract on the company's server.

- *Suggest a scenario and ask, "What would happen if...?"* This will help you verify how well the process is controlled if there is a deviation or if something goes wrong. It will also help you assess the effectiveness of communication and awareness of authority and responsibility. Does the person know what he or she is authorized to handle, and what incidents require input from a supervisor?

- *Ask what happens next.* Avoid quality speak. If you're trying to determine what the output of a process is, simply ask, "What happens next?" Asking a customer service technician, "What's the output of the process?" will probably get you a blank stare followed by an awkward moment in which you'll get the sense that you've just made him or her feel incompetent—which isn't the case. The technician knows perfectly well that when the order is entered in the database, it next gets routed to the scheduler, who confirms the ship date so that the order can then be acknowledged to the customer.

- *Ask "why?"* People who do tasks mindlessly, without understanding the reason for the activity, are less likely to be diligent in ensuring that the process is consistently and correctly implemented. It's hard to care about something that makes no sense.

- *Give the process owner time to answer.* Be patient. He or she may be thinking. Don't assume that a delayed response is an indication that the person is lying or making stuff up.

- *Don't be afraid to repeat or restate your question.* Sometimes we need to come at a subject from a different angle. Restating a question helps the auditee to grasp what you're trying to ascertain. In this case it's helpful to communicate to the auditee that it is your shortcoming in not asking the right question—and not his or hers—for being unable to comprehend what you're trying to ask.

- *Write down the answer so you don't forget.* Always record the evidence you've assessed. Take copious notes. It helps with follow-up questions. It has the additional benefit of providing the foundation for the audit report and allays any confrontation. The auditor doesn't need to defend his or her conclusion. All that's needed is a reference to the evidence upon which the observation is based.

- *If you're writing while the person is speaking, make sure that he or she knows it.* Say, "I'm listening to you, but I need to write this down." If you get the sense that the auditee is afraid that your report will result in punitive action, explain why you write things down. My favorite line goes something like this: "I have a brain like a sieve. If I don't write things down, I'll forget, and I won't be able to do my report."

Another consideration when interviewing is the need to be simultaneously observing activities, records, and the work environment.

I had occasion recently to observe an auditor in a non-auditing setting. It was interesting to note the manner in which he carried on conversations with various people during an informal meeting. Whomever he spoke with received his undivided attention. The transition in focus as the conversation moved back and forth among the meeting members was subtle. His head shifted slightly, his eyes focusing on the new speaker as he re-directed his attention.

There was never a hint of boredom or distraction. I was struck by this man's relaxed and yet respectful demeanor. I realized that I was observing one of the finest qualities of a good auditor.

The output of an audit, i.e., the audit report, is based upon observation. What do we observe and how do we observe it? What does the manner in which we scrutinize documents, records, finished goods, and other evidence communicate to the auditee? Do we register skepticism or disdain? Do our eyes glaze over revealing distraction or disinterest? Or, do we glare at the auditee, creating an atmosphere of intimidation or feigned superiority? Do our eyes refute our claim of objectivity?

In some cultures sustained eye contact is considered invasive and disrespectful, but in the vast majority of social settings, eye contact communicates interest and responsiveness. It's deemed an expression of open candor. It encourages further discourse and alleviates tension. And, so, looking directly at the person with whom you are speaking is by and large the most effective technique for conducting an audit interview.

Auditors must also spend time observing the environment in which processes are conducted. They must be able to assess if the work space and general infrastructure are appropriate for the work being done. Is it clean and well lit? Are tools easily accessible? Are there distractions or safety concerns that will interfere with the process or affect the product? Are there particular environmental requirements related to the industry—humidity control, special garbing protocols, or hazardous material containment?

Auditors are also required to assess support processes, such as calibration. Is the micrometer calibration current? Does the preventive maintenance tag hanging from the side of the CNC machine indicate if the preventive maintenance has been done as scheduled? Are parts properly tagged for traceability? Auditors must be observant. This is an example of systems approach in action—seeing how everything fits together and contributes to the desired output.

How can an auditor balance these two disparate needs: to focus on the auditees' responses and to assess the evidence and environment in which the processes are being conducted?

Auditors must be fully present to the individuals they are interviewing. This means that the auditor's attention is deliberately focused on the auditee. He or she is neither distracted nor pre-occupied. The person being interviewed is entitled to the auditor's undivided and respectful attention. This is non-negotiable. No auditee should ever be made to feel that the auditor's questions are superfluous or that his or her answers are unimportant. The benefit is twofold: this demeanor decreases tension and it ensures more accurate and complete responses.

So, how to ensure that all the other observations about tools and infrastructure requirements get handled? This is just another of the skills auditors must hone. They need to develop a sensitivity to the pauses and rhythms of the interview and to recognize moments to glance over at machines and tools. Subtle opportunities arise to assess and observe while an auditee is searching for a document or when your conversation is interrupted by an important phone call. Auditors also need to identify the right moment in the question sequence to say, "I'd like to take a few minutes to look over these records, or ID tags, or warehouse configuration..."

Finally, it's important to reiterate that the audit interview is not a normal everyday activity for the auditee. As long as I've been auditing and consulting, I've seen competent, intelligent people morph into blithering, jittering half-wits in the presence of auditors. They forget where to find documents. They miss steps in processes they've been performing for years. They babble on about what they think other people do. Or they just stare off into space with their mouths agape, creating the impression that they're either praying for divine intervention or for Scotty to beam them up and out of this mess.

It's easy for an auditor to say, "Relax; don't worry." We underestimate the sinking feelings of confusion, embarrassment, and, ultimately, regret auditees experience after the auditor walks away. They say, "I wish I'd told her about the new form that makes tracking easier" or "I didn't do a very good job of explaining how this works."

Intellectually, auditees may know there is nothing to fear, but that knowledge doesn't diminish the sensation of dread or inadequacy. Auditors' cavalier platitudes about not worrying come off as dismissive, rather than reassuring.

There's not much auditors can do to eliminate the negative feelings. People are either afraid of the auditor because they know processes aren't operating the way they should or because they take pride in their work and want to ensure that the auditor fully appreciates the organization's achievements.

So what can auditors do to ameliorate the problem? They can be a bit more judicious in the selection of their words. They can be more careful in the manner in which they ask questions. Often the tongue-tied stupor that numbs an auditee's tongue is the result of unexpected questions or questions that seem accusatory rather than thought provoking. Auditors can amplify their ability to discern when very competent people are simply nervous, regardless of the auditor's attempts at reassurance. Auditors need to remind themselves that the purpose of an audit is to gather objective evidence on the status of conformance to a defined set of requirements. It's fact finding, not fault finding.

From time to time, we all have a deer-in-the-headlights moment. That's that mortifying sensation you get when you seem incapable of uttering a single coherent sentence. Again, remember that the auditees were not hired to answer your questions. You just to need to cut them some slack and help them relax.

All of us, auditors and quality professionals alike, can strive to cultivate organizational cultures that reflect the objective fact-finding benchmark we need to achieve to have successful and effective audit programs. We need to internalize W. Edwards Deming's most important point: "Drive out fear!"

Although these tactics may at first feel contrived, if they're practiced regularly, they will eventually become second nature. The result will be a more respectful audit experience for both the auditor and the auditee, and a more productive audit result for the organization.

# CHAPTER 6

# Manage the Audit Team

W e spend a lot of time talking about the individual auditor's role, responsibilities, activities, etc. But we don't devote sufficient time to discussing the importance of how the audit team works together.

It's indisputable that auditor competence is the most essential factor affecting the outcome of the audit process. And, we can readily concede that a significant portion of audits are carried out by the solo lead auditor. But, where there's a need for multiple auditors, challenges must be addressed to ensure an effective audit.

The concept of teamwork is more than just a euphemistic nicety. Interactions between auditors, sharing of tasks and information, and decisions about what will go into the final report all contribute to ensuring a balanced audit that will achieve its purpose: to ensure conformance to an identified standard, to assess effectiveness, and to provide opportunities to correct the cause of problems and experience improvement.

What factors go into a successful audit team performance?

As was discussed earlier developing the audit plan is not terribly difficult, but it can be time consuming and laborious. Despite that fact, it's a fundamental and indispensable contributor to team performance.

When there's only one auditor the only constraints on the schedule may be the availability of the auditees. Development of the audit plan for an audit team is markedly different. The plan must ensure that the workload is evenly assigned—that each auditor's allotted time allows for adequate assessment. It's a simple matter of proportionate allocation of resources. Care must be taken to ensure that two auditors aren't scheduled to interview the same person at the same time. For example, in smaller companies some people wear multiple hats. If the president of the company is also the purchasing agent, there's no way that management review and purchasing can be audited at the same time.

There are some other important considerations that rarely get mentioned. For example, as self-evident as it might seem, auditors need to be reminded that their notes must be legible. When there's only one auditor, it's not as critical. Generally, most of us can read our own handwriting. But, if you're the lead assessor in an audit team of three, you need to be able to read everyone else's notes to be able to generate the audit report. Conversely, if you're one of the other team members, the lead auditor is relying on you to take complete and intelligible notes. Without them, the audit report will be skewed toward only the findings that can actually be read.

Lunch breaks and end-of-day recaps should be used to compare notes and to review how the audit as a whole is going. Concerns should be aired—even minor ones. Sometimes, minor glitches that would normally receive passing notice in a report could be presumed to be isolated anomalies. During the audit team meeting, it might be discovered that comparable glitches have been observed in various areas. Processes that permeate the entire organization such as document control and record retention are two likely candidates for observing systemwide issues. One auditor will have looked at purchasing documents and found the appended specifications aren't always the latest revision. A second auditor may have observed that field service contracts aren't controlled when a client makes changes. A third auditor might note that engineering change notices aren't handled in accordance with documented requirements. Taken individually, each incident could be taken as a minor nonconformance. However, taken together they could reveal a systemic breakdown of a core process—i.e., document control. Depending on the industry and the risk inherent, this could warrant a major finding of nonconformity. This fact might not come to light if each auditor individually assumed he or she was dealing with a minor anomaly that wasn't worthy of a finding.

In the absence of an end-of-day recap, the audit team might miss the fact that scattered anomalies reveal a systemic breakdown in the organization's document control processes. For an internal audit, since the audits are generally shorter in duration, this re-cap might take place at lunch time or even during a break.

The opposite scenario is equally likely. The information gathered from one auditor may answer the concern raised by another team member, preventing the erroneous citing of a nonconformance. Discussions may reveal that the auditee has a nontraditional method of controlling a certain process. For example, the production supervisor may be responsible for qualifying suppliers of outsourced processes or daily production schedules could be documented on a white board and controlled throughout the facility with color-coded tags on bins—no printed schedule and no traveler or router accompanying the job.

This leads me to my next point. Auditors must communicate effectively with one another. They should be able to comprehend the interrelation between a set of processes they are auditing and those being assessed by another team member. What happens in one area often affects what happens in another. One of the quality management principles relates to a systems approach to managing the quality management system (QMS). Auditors should always apply this approach, but it's more challenging when there are multiple auditors. Everything is connected. What has been observed by one auditor may create an audit trail that needs to be picked up by another member of the team. If, for example, traceability of materials in the stock room is reliant on information requested during purchasing, the members of the team looking at these two processes have to compare the results of their unique assessments. And, if traceability flows all the way through the manufacturing or installation processes, the trail needs to be followed to its ultimate conclusion. The evidence of serialization or lot number traceability could run from the initial request from the customer through various processes from purchasing to receipt to warehousing to kitting to manufacturing or assembly to shipping or installation to final retention of the records. Because multiple auditors will be observing different segments of this trail, they need to share information to efficiently assess the effectiveness of traceability practices.

So far we've dealt largely with audit teams whose members work independently coming together only for the opening meeting, periodic recaps, and the closing meeting. This is very common in second- and third-party audits but can also occur in first-party (internal) audits—especially with larger organizations.

In other instances, audit teams may operate in pairs. There are several benefits to working with one other auditor. It tends to amplify the results of the audit. Having two sets of eyes and ears increases the level of objectivity. It's easier to pare away unintentional biases when a second observer articulates what has been observed. Two auditors can prompt one another on important questions, decreasing the likelihood that a significant factor gets missed. Finally, as long as they don't have an accusatory attitude, the interview takes on more of the feel of a conversation. Unfortunately, if both auditors are coming off as interrogators, the audit ends up sounding like something out of The Inquisition.

It's a good idea to plan ahead of time who will cover what areas—who will ask what questions. Regardless of which auditor asks a question, it's important for both of them to record the responses and to write down what evidence was assessed. We all occasionally forget to write something down, so this method ensures good backup and full coverage in most instances.

Finally, the team should speak with one voice to the auditee. If, for example, a major nonconformance has been uncovered during the course of the audit, the responsibility for informing management resides with the lead auditor—and no one else. Otherwise the audit takes on the air of a gossip-mongering conduit. Individual members of the audit team should contribute their assessment of any issue and work with the lead auditor to arrive at a conclusion. However, the lead auditor is the one who has the responsibility for conclusions and findings that are disclosed during the exit meeting or included in the audit report. The integrity of the entire audit is undermined if the report conflicts with information that an individual auditor has prematurely or separately communicated to the auditee.

When it comes to auditing, teamwork isn't just a matter of making sure everything gets covered. The team's expertise, judgment, and audit skills are pooled as a shared asset to ensure that the client gets the most benefit from their shared effort.

# CHAPTER 7

# Write Informative
# Audit Reports

The audit report is the product of the audit. Without it the audit is incomplete. The information contained in the report will be used by others to make decisions that affect the entire organization. It provides insight into what processes and functions are working well, perceptions of risk, and identification of what has gone wrong. From these insights will flow corrective actions, preventive actions, lean initiatives, benchmarking activities, and an array of improvement projects.

Internal audits are essential inputs into the management review process. Some of the decisions that occur during strategic planning may be a direct result of audit findings. Therefore, what goes into the report matters.

As with other chapters, the primary focus is internal auditing. However, it's appropriate to make a brief comment about supplier audits. Any time an auditor conducts a supplier audit, it's appropriate to send the supplier (or potential supplier) an audit report. It's unfair to only send a list of requests for corrective action. The organization has extended you the courtesy of its time and deserves to experience the benefit of a complete assessment report. A supplier audit report contains information that will be used to decide whether the company will be added to the approved supplier list. Additionally, it may contain information about capacity, unique processes, or areas of concern that may need to be addressed either through corrective actions or through a joint improvement project with your organization.

The essential fact to keep in mind is that the audit report needs to be informative and it must provide value. It's important to write a comprehensive audit report. The report doesn't have to be lengthy, but it should convey a balanced summary of the status of the organization audited. It should mention good practices that have been observed, risks that have been perceived, and problems that have been identified.

The internal audit report should include the following information. (Again, supplier or third-party audits should contain comparable information.)

- *Date of the audit.* When did the audit take place? This provides evidence that audits are being conducted in accordance with the established audit schedule. Frequent lapses in the schedule may be indicative of an erosion in the organization's commitment to the internal auditing program. It might also reflect a problem in terms of resources. Are auditors being told by their supervisors that they can't take time from their regular jobs? This might suggest a devaluation of the process by some middle managers. Or, it may simply be that there aren't enough auditors in the audit pool and it's impossible to get the audits done within the allotted time.

  Another factor to consider is one of practicality. Auditing is an auditable quality management system (QMS) function. Your registrar or some other third-party assessor needs to verify that audits are being conducted in accordance with the plan and that audit conclusions are based on adequate objective evidence.

  It's also appropriate to record the duration of the audit. This helps top management get a clear picture of the resources that are being expended. How much time and money is the organization spending on internal auditing? This can be weighed against the cost-saving problem solving that resulted from good audit findings.

- *Areas audited.* For an internal audit in a small company, this would be as simple as saying what departments were visited. However, a larger company could have an expansive campus with several buildings or multiple locations. In either of these cases, it's important to record the location, especially if there are findings that the organization may wish to investigate further to see if they are localized or systemic. Conversely, if good practices are observed, it helps with being able to benchmark them later so that they can be applied in other parts of the organization. There's also the possibility that an activity is conducted at more than one site so it would be important to ensure that the other sites are audited at a later date in the audit cycle.

- *Standard used.* For a third-party audit, it's a QMS standard such as ISO 9001, ISO/TS 16949, ISO 13485, etc. For internal audits, it's usually a list of the internal documents associated with the functions and activities audited. Examples would include procedures and work instructions. In some organizations, the auditors are also asked to verify conformance to the applicable management system standard, so they would include reference to the applicable standard, for example ISO 9001:2008. When referencing the standard, it's appropriate to include the revision year.

- *Lead auditor and audit team members.* Every team has a lead auditor. If there's only one auditor, that person is the lead auditor. That individual has the ultimate responsibility for generating the audit report. Other team members must be listed in the report, along with any technical experts who may have accompanied the team. They serve to provide very specific technical information that may exceed the knowledge of any of the auditors. These individuals generally aren't used for internal audits unless the organization has some highly specialized processes.

    Bearing in mind again that the audit process itself gets audited, having the names of the interviewees allows the auditor to confirm that none of the internal auditors audited their own work. When conducting surveillance audits I regularly ask what functions the auditors have in the company and compare them against the scope of the audits they have conducted.

- *Persons interviewed.* This provides evidence that the persons who answered questions were actually the process owners who have responsibility for the activity. It's not uncommon for people to try to be helpful and answer an auditor's question even if it's not part of their regular job. Sometimes the auditor finds out too late that he or she wasn't speaking to the right person. During a closing meeting you may hear a manager say something like, "Francine doesn't take care of patient intake, so she wouldn't know where those forms are kept." As awkward as it is for the auditor, it's best to find out even this late in the process, so that corrections can be made and unwarranted findings of nonconformance can be removed.

  Recording the names of persons interviewed helps auditors provide objective evidence that they've fulfilled the requirements of the auditing process.

- *Good points.* An audit isn't an attempt to amass a collection of bad events. Therefore, an audit report should also mention good points that were observed. "A newly developed software program is facilitating communication between departments on new projects," "The records show evidence that operators have had training on the ERP system that was introduced three months ago," or "The corrective action tracking system is better able to calculate the cost of nonconformities and the money saved when problems are solved." These are all examples of positive comments an auditor might have observed. They serve as an objective indication that resources allocated are showing return on investment.

  It's also nice to acknowledge accomplishments and success stories. People are so accustomed to only hearing about the dreaded "NCs" that they don't want to read the audit reports—much less appreciate them as opportunities to make things better. It's gratifying to hear: "Well done."

- *Observations (also called opportunities for improvement and often abbreviated OFI).* It's appropriate for auditors to make statements about perceptions of risk or the identification of a process that may not be controlled as well as it should be to prevent problems. They shouldn't specifically say something is wrong, but they should intimate what might go wrong. Examples might include: "It was observed that the router for fast-turnaround jobs does not provide adequate instruction for certain steps, which could result in errors and defective products needing to be reworked" or "Nonconforming material waiting to be scrapped is stored in close proximity to customer property. Even though the material is tagged, there is a risk of the customer product being accidentally discarded." Again, in each example, there is no nonconformance. There is, however, the risk that something could easily happen which could result in a problem or nonconformance.

- *Nonconformities.* ISO 9000:2005—Fundamentals and vocabulary—defines a nonconformity as: "a nonfulfillment of a requirement." When writing up findings of nonconformity, it's important to be clear and complete. What is the actual nonconformity? What is the requirement? What evidence did you use to conclude that there was a nonconformity?

    Let's take each one of these in turn.

  o *What is the nonconformity?* This should be a clear, unbiased statement of fact. For example, "The inspection records provide evidence that material was accepted that exceeded the allowable tolerance range" or "There are no records to provide evidence that the report was reviewed by an authorized reviewer before being submitted to the client." Note that in neither case is there an accusatory tone or assignment of blame. In neither finding is it stated that a specific individual did something wrong. It's important to refrain from using people's names when writing up a finding of nonconformity. Also, remember that you can't report what you have not observed. It would not be appropriate to say: "Michael passed material through that was out of spec" or "The report wasn't reviewed." You didn't see the operator accept defective product and you don't know that the report wasn't reviewed, only that there's no record.

It's important to be starkly factual. It's possible that there was an engineering deviation issued and so the issue isn't with Michael, but with the function that was responsible for providing the record of the deviation. And, the report could have been reviewed and approved using a new electronic signature that hasn't yet been documented in the procedure. In both cases, something isn't right. The manner in which you write it up will determine if they'll chock it up to "operator error" and "re-train the operator." Or, if someone will ask why there was an error and look for the true cause, thereby preventing recurrence—or escalation to a more serious occurrence next time.

This isn't the time to suggest solutions or to presume to know the cause. The statement should not include language that says, "We should try doing this _____" or "Because the document revisions weren't distributed..." The audit is an objective factual account. What ensues from the audit report is up to someone else.

○ *What is the requirement?* It's inappropriate—wrong, actually—to write up a finding of nonconformity that can't be tied to a requirement. Without a requirement, all an auditor has is something he or she doesn't like—and it's irrelevant to the audit report. This justifies the finding. For the first example, the requirement is found in the customer specification. When citing a document, the auditor must be specific. The statement of requirement might read: "Drawing 7878993, Rev. F, calls out a tolerance of 9.75" +/- 0.005".The records indicate that the parts accepted measured 9.68." For the second example: "Procedure 8.2.4, Rev. C, specifies in section 7.7 that all reports must be reviewed by a second independent reviewer and that the reviewer must sign and date the last page of the report." Details like revision levels are also important. They sometimes shine a light on the fact that people don't have the right information—steering the investigation away from the unfortunate and ubiquitous "operator error" root cause.

Having specific information as to the requirement provides several benefits. It demonstrates why there is a nonconformance. This, in turn, dispels any confrontations as to the legitimacy of the finding. And, finally, it helps to launch the root cause analysis when it comes time to investigate the problem.

o *What is the evidence?* The third factor to include is the evidence that substantiates the finding. For the first it would be Inspection Report #15549 from August 30; for the other it would be the Service Report #546 from September 15. This reinforces the justification for the finding and also facilitates the root cause analysis process.

An additional factor can be added if it's deemed appropriate. I call it the "So What?" factor. This is a brief statement of the reason this problem needs to be addressed. With both of the examples given it would be appropriate to say that the risk is that customers will get defective product. Other concerns might include timely rework or possible regulatory action.

For most audit reports there should be fewer findings of nonconformity than good things or opportunities for improvement.

The last thing to put into the report would be the results of any verification of open corrective actions. This can relate back to earlier statements about improvements that have been observed. Because the audit function owns responsibility for ensuring action is taken on audit findings, this efficient method serves to close the loop on previous audits.

The auditor's working papers (checklist, notes, samples, and closed out corrective actions) should be either appended to the report or available for review.

Following these basic audit practices should ensure that the information management gets is accurate, reflects the status of the organization, and is detailed enough so that it results in good decisions. This is what makes audits effective. Anything less is a meaningless paper shuffle.

# CHAPTER 8

# Take Action on Audit Findings

Audit reports should result in actions, otherwise there wouldn't be much point in doing them. It's typical for audit findings of non-conformity to generate either corrective actions or simple corrections. Opportunities for improvement (OFIs) and positive findings should prompt preventive actions and other improvement initiatives.

If there's no useful or useable information coming out of the audit report, the whole audit process is a waste of time. There are organizations that believe that zero findings is a desirable goal. Some even make it one of their quality objectives. Here's the problem with that reasoning. It's not unlikely to have an occasional audit with no findings of nonconformity. However, having repeat audits with no findings means that the auditors aren't doing their jobs. No organization is perfect. Things change with unanticipated consequences. A seemingly minor glitch happens and we don't react proportionately. There's turnover in personnel. New technology is acquired. Suppliers go out of business and have to be replaced. The list is endless. With so many dynamics and the constancy of change, it's nearly impossible to never have anything go wrong.

At the very least, there should be some observable OFIs. These perceptions of risk can be used to launch *kaizen* events, lean initiatives, and preventive actions. My personal experience is that it is in this category that organizations garner the greatest benefit from the internal audit program. Fixing existing problems is mandatory. But, identifying risks, anticipating problems, and taking action before the costs and negative consequences erupt is an infinitely more beneficial pursuit. The further upstream a problem is identified, the less pain is experienced by the organization. So, identifying a potential problem in the design process reduces the risk of financial loss further down the line at the manufacturing stage or at the client's location.

The last category, dealing with observations of excellent or improved processes or features, can also initiate improvements. If a great idea that was launched in one facility has proven to be successful, management might decide to try the idea at other locations. When the audit report was discussed in chapter 7, it was mentioned that auditors should be involved in verifying the effects of corrective actions. If the report indicates that the corrective action has not only prevented recurrence of a problem but has also improved workflow, the organization has the objective evidence it needs to justify deployment of similar actions in other departments.

It's important to identify who decides what actions will be taken. There are various things to consider: What observations require action, what kind of action should be taken, and who will be assigned the action?

Some things are easier to decide than others. There are several steps and possible directions that can be taken.

Who reviews the audit report? The first person to review the report is probably the manager of the audit program. This is generally the quality manager or an individual who serves in a comparable position. The first area to examine are the nonconformities, because they require action. The quality manager may decide how to proceed without consulting anyone. In some cases, the course of action is so clear that it requires little discussion. But in many cases there are factors to consider before initiating a corrective action. ISO 9001:2008, section 8.5.2, states: "Corrective actions shall be appropriate to the effects of the nonconformities encountered."

Not everything warrants corrective action. There is a reasonable alternative. ISO 9000:2005 identifies two possible courses. It differentiates between correction and corrective action. Correction is defined as "action to eliminate a detected nonconformity." Corrective action is defined as "action to eliminate the cause of a detected nonconformity."

There may be findings of nonconformity in the audit report that don't warrant corrective action. If there is one document that has not been revised, the best action may be to simply complete the revision and move on. Similarly, if a sampling of five reports showed that one did not have a required signature, it might be acceptable to get the signature and remind the reviewers of the correct procedure. This decision is reliant on the level of risk. If the missing signature is a regulatory requirement or carries legal significance, then the appropriate decision might be to initiate corrective action.

Because many of the decisions are complex, requiring an understanding of the effects of the nonconformity as well as criteria for determining risk, it's appropriate to solicit the input of other individuals. The quality manager should not be deciding in a vacuum what things warrant corrective action and to whom they should be assigned. Although quality managers have a holistic view of the organization, they don't have expertise in all areas. And, having the quality manager as the sole arbiter of what justifies corrective action and who should be involved, perpetuates the silo view within the organization that the quality function owns complete decision-making responsibility for the output of audits. That's unfortunate and shortsighted. It creates the impression that the audit process is just about fulfilling an ISO requirement and has nothing to do with the business of the company. It devalues the audit process and engenders the risk that the whole program will degrade into a paper-pushing exercise because it produces no meaningful outcomes.

Therefore, the quality manager, with input from various other functions decides if a finding of nonconformance will be handled through simple correction or through more extensive corrective action.

This decision should be recorded for each action. How it gets recorded is a matter of choice and efficiency. Some organizations use an audit report form that allows for tracking actions directly on the form. This helps with traceability and ensures that even small actions don't get lost. However, it means that if the action taken is a corrective action, there has to be effective linkage to the corrective action process to ensure that the ultimate outcome gets looped back to the audit report. Other organizations use a separate spreadsheet or a software package to manage corrections, corrective actions, preventive actions, and other improvement activities.

Once the decision has been made, the actions should be promptly assigned. This reiterates the need for several individuals to participate in the decisions around initiating corrective action. Without additional input, it's not uncommon for the corrective action to be assigned to the individual closest to the point of detection. This often results in root cause analysis that remains within that one department or function. Because many problems have systemic elements, this siloed approach can result in an incorrect determination of root cause—and a repetition of the problem.

The outputs of the actions need to be tracked. For those that take longer to implement, it's appropriate to have a mechanism for periodic monitoring. It's important to ensure that actions are implemented. Otherwise, we're back to the concern about the value of the audit process.

Because nonconformities always require some kind of action, the records are usually not too difficult to find.

OFIs pose different challenges. They generally suggest a level of risk. The decision as to what action to take, if any, is more complex. The quality manager, as the first reviewer of the audit report, may decide that some OFIs should be addressed immediately and will consult with other managers as to what action to take. But there are others that may require aggregation of additional trending data or a more thorough investigation of the cost versus the risk. In some instances, the decision may be tabled until a management review meeting, allowing top management to opine on the merits of the observation. If there are several OFIs on one audit report, there may be consideration of prioritization. A decision may be made to wait to see if the situation stabilizes or if other factors mitigate the risk. Managers could assess an OFI and decide that there is no appreciable risk and that it would be inappropriate to take action.

Preventive actions are one of the most effective methods of addressing OFIs. The actions themselves may take many forms such as failure mode and effects analysis (FMEA), increased monitoring, preventive mainte-nance, or more formalized risk management procedures. What they all have in common is the ability to address issues before they become non-conformities.

All decisions taken, including the decision to take no action, should be recorded. This is helpful in preventing the re-hashing of concerns that have already been discussed. It also provides evidence that there has been deliberation of the observations.

Actions resulting from good comments are probably most effectively handled through the management review process. These and the preven-tive actions may involve strategic planning and capital expenditure, which are the direct responsibility of top management.

There should be follow-up of all actions taken to fulfill the intent of the audit program and to close the loop on the audit cycle. Complete and concise follow-up of actions resulting from internal audits facilitates re-porting back to management on the internal audit program. It helps to highlight the success stories as well as the challenges the organization faces.

# CHAPTER 9

# Report Back to Top Management

Top management needs good information to make good decisions. One of the sources of this information is the internal audit program.

There's an implicit reciprocity within the organization when it comes to internal auditing. Top management provides resources for the program in the form of people, training, and time. There may be an additional provision of software to manage the process, including scheduling, notification, linkage to corrective actions, etc., or space for prep, meetings, and audit report writing.

Internal auditing is like any other process in your organization. Just as with the other processes, there are requirements for people, documents, planning, tools, etc. And, again, just as with any other process, top management has the ultimate responsibility for ensuring that the resources are provided and that the process is implemented.

Top management also provides something else that is equally valuable and necessary. They offer their commitment and their visible and vocal support of the program. Through their attitude they convey the respect they have for the auditors' work. And, they make it clear to middle-management that this program is important and, therefore, auditors must be allowed adequate time to prepare for the audits, to conduct them effectively, and to generate their reports.

The simple fact is that good managers don't—and shouldn't—ask their people to support bad programs. It's difficult for an executive to make the case for auditing if his or her attitude suggests that he or she has no respect for the process and no commitment to using any of the information that comes out of the audit report. When audit reports are poorly written, clearly illustrating that the auditors have done a shoddy job, responsible leaders are loathe to ask middle-managers and supervisors to support the audit program. It's impossible and inappropriate for them to champion a process that they resent as a waste of time and resources.

Auditors reciprocate management's commitment to the program and its provision of resources by conducting effective audits in a professional manner and by writing concise reports filled with useful information. They justify the investment that leadership has made in them and the audit program.

Most quality management system (QMS) models require review of audits as a component of the management review process. The question is: What should go into the review?

I've seen records of management review where the topic of internal audits was encapsulated in one bullet: "4 audits performed in last 6 months." So what? Who cares? In ISO 9001 and in similar sector-derived standards the actual requirement is to review the "results of audits."

What results of audits might be of interest to top management?
- The status of the organization
- Problems that have been resolved
- Problems that remain unresolved—or that required corrective action
- Risks that have been identified
- Opportunities for improvement (OFIs)
- Effectiveness of actions from previous audits

Let's take each one of these in turn.

## The status of the organization

There are multiple indicators that top management uses to take the pulse of the organization: key performance indicators, dashboards, analysis of statistical process control data, customer feedback, etc. All of these taken together are used to patch together a portrait of the company. Taken individually, they can be skewed or present an incomplete picture. The key performance indicators may show an improvement in first-pass yield. As a stand-alone factoid it doesn't mean much. But, an auditor might add that during the course of the audit, it was observed that the process has been significantly streamlined through a recently conducted *kaizen* event without affecting throughput. The process continues to be controlled in accordance with regulatory requirements. The auditors were able to observe objectively that it was possible to experience efficiency without compromising product quality.

These kinds of observations add texture to the report and other data being presented during the management review. It shows not only what improved but also how it improved.

Sometimes the audit reports provide simple confirmation that the system is working as it should and that the company is not in danger of falling out of compliance with mandatory regulatory requirements.

## Problems that have been resolved

During the course of audits issues may arise that require simple correction. Document revisions may not have been updated on the master document list. One training record didn't find its way into the appropriate files. These are anomalies that carry no appreciable risk. Bearing in mind the ISO 9001:2008 requirement in 8.5.2 that states: "Corrective action shall be appropriate to the effects of the nonconformities encountered," it makes perfect sense that some things can be resolved through simple correction.

It would be inefficient to cite all the mistakes that have been fixed through correction. But it might be worth a few words to contrast these findings with the select few that did result in corrective actions. This serves to reassure management that there is some semblance of a vetting process that goes into initiating corrective actions and that the organization isn't being forced to waste resources on every small hiccup in the system.

It's also a subtle reminder that what sometimes starts out as stray anomalies can evolve into a troublesome trend.

## Problems that required corrective action—or that remain unresolved

The least pleasant items to review would be the nonconformances (NC) that show where the organization is failing to meet requirements, which puts it at greatest risk of not meeting customer and/or regulatory requirements. Management needs to know about these problems. Leadership must have objective, unbiased information about the problems so that appropriate decisions can be made. Just because a corrective action has been initiated that doesn't mean the issue can be swept under the rug.

Again, as with the corrections mentioned earlier and depending on the size and complexity of the QMS, it might not be appropriate to mention all the NCs found during an audit cycle. It might be worth summarizing them and highlighting the ones that pose the greatest risk to the organization.

There are also some instances when corrective actions cannot be initiated without deliberation and authorization from top management.

Top managers need to know what audit findings save the company from embarrassment, financial loss, or litigation. A nonconformity identified in the design-and-development process could be a life safer. Handling this corrective action is infinitely cheaper than dealing with it either at the production level or after the product has been delivered to the customer.

---

# Risks that have been identified

Risks, unlike actual nonconformances, indicate a probability that something might go wrong—that there's a potential for a problem. Not all potential problems require action.

Once risks have been enumerated and explained, top management has the necessary information to decide what items warrant action. Because resources are limited, they also have the latitude to prioritize actions based upon availability of resources weighed against the criticality of perceived risks.

Through the information provided in their reports, auditors illuminate these issues and facilitate management's deliberation process.

---

# Opportunities for improvement

OFIs have a lot in common with the previous category of identified risks. In both instances, no nonconformance has been cited.

However, unlike those observations that focus primarily on risk, there are other observations that might be indicative of inefficiency or limited effectiveness. There is an element of risk, but it's more attuned to loss of time, wasted steps, obsolete technology, or practices that have not evolved with changing times.

In actuality, all of the actions resulting from categories discussed so far carry with them the opportunity for improvement.

Every time an auditor writes up an OFI, he or she is presenting the organization a golden chance to prevent a bad thing from happening or to mitigate some form of financial loss through inadequacy or inefficiency. Risk-based thinking and risk management are increasing in importance in all management systems in all fields and industries. Properly reviewed, management can deliberate over each, decide which warrant action, and prioritize them in accordance with the level of risk and the available resources. This is another way of looking at return on investment (ROI).

The OFI category above all others makes the financial case for the internal audit program because it demonstrates forward thinking, planning, and choice. Top management chooses to listen to the wisdom of the auditor and uses the information to mitigate risk and improve the organization.

## Effectiveness of actions from previous audits

Actions resulting from previous reviews are another item on the list that can serve to provide perspective over time. "These were the issues we had in the past. This is how they were dealt with. Things have significantly improved."

What else should management hear?

They should have a sense of how much money the auditing program is contributing to the bottom line. Some of this will tie into the review of corrective actions and preventive actions. It's unavoidable and actually reflective of the systems approach to management. Everything is connected.

What metrics would raise eyebrows during a management review?

- Number of findings that were resolved, resulting in a decrease in defects, labor-intensive re-works, employee overtime hours, and customer complaints. Even though this is often linked to corrective action metrics, it's appropriate to give a summation with a note that some issues will be discussed in greater detail during the corrective action portion of the review.
- Hours spent auditing and number of auditors. Some organizations monetize individuals' work by the hours spent on a given project or task. So, if there are six auditors who average ten hours per month

auditing (including prep and report writing) and the hourly rate ascribed to the audit task is $40 per hour, the total annual expenditure would be about $29,000. But, if the actions that ensued from the audit findings each save the company about $10,000, and there are 15 during the course of one year, the company ends up saving more than $100,000. That's a pretty good ROI.

The ROI can't happen if management doesn't provide the resources and if auditors don't perform effective audits. The review of results of audits during the management review process provide the top executives the rationale they need to continue to support the audit program because it has demonstrated its value to the bottom line.

# CHAPTER 10

# Conclusion

Internal audits are an indisputably necessary component of any successful management system. Without effective audits organizations miss an essential opportunity to assess how the processes that enable them to serve their customers are working.

The nine essential steps presented in this book provide the foundation to achieving the goal of having an effective and financially justifiable audit program.

1. *Plan and prepare.*

   Make sure that you plan your audit program taking into account the unique characteristics and constraints of your organization. Don't toss together a quick generic schedule. Make sure that in planning the audits that you ensure auditor objectivity.

   Give auditors time to develop checklists and to prepare adequately for the audits.

2. *Drive fear out of the audit program.*

   Strip your audit program of any suggestion of intimidation or punitive action. Cultivate a culture where audits are perceived as positive activities.

Avoid setting a quality objective of zero audit findings. It just drives problems underground as people strive to achieve an inappropriate goal.

3. *Ensure adequate training.*

There is never a good excuse for using untrained auditors. You wouldn't use untrained inspectors or machinists. Well-trained auditors provide useful information through the utilization of proven audit techniques. They also conduct themselves in a manner that reflects the highest intent of the audit program.

4. *Create effective checklists.*

Create and use checklists that facilitate a thorough and effective audit experience. Good checklists contribute to time management and more meaningful audit findings.

Avoid using checklists with Yes/No columns. They limit the information that comes out of the audit.

5. *Hone your interviewing skills.*

Good interviewing skills don't come naturally to everyone. But, the skills can be learned and honed over time. Use proven techniques for asking questions and listening to the responses.

Always bear in mind that auditees were not hired to answer auditors' questions. They're hired to do their jobs. They should be able to explain what they do—and the onus is upon the auditors to illicit responses that demonstrate their competence and conformity to defined requirements.

6. *Manage the audit team.*

Audit teams need to work together to ensure that systemic issues are not discounted as scattered anomalies. The lead auditor should direct the team and make adjustments to tasks if the need arises. As with any other team, the team members need to communicate effectively.

7. *Write an informative audit report.*

Write a balanced and objective audit report. Make sure to include positive comments, perceived risks, and any findings of nonconformity. Use the notes from the audit to support the audit conclusions.

8. *Take action on audit findings.*

The audit function owns responsibility for the close-out of actions that result from audit findings. Ensure that actions are taken and conduct follow-up either during subsequent audits or as a separate verification.

9. *Report back to top management.*

Honor the commitment and support that management has invested in the audit program. Provide top management with audit reports that create value.

And, finally, make the financial case for the audit program. The ultimate effectiveness of an audit program can be found in the data that demonstrates the return on investment.

# ABOUT THE AUTHOR

Denise Robitaille is the author of numerous books on various quality topics. She is an internationally recognized speaker who brings years of experience in business and industry to her work in the quality profession. Denise is an active member of the U.S. TAG to ISO/TC 176, the committee responsible for updating the ISO 9000 family of standards. She is also an Exemplar Global-certified lead assessor, an ASQ Certified Quality Auditor, and a fellow of ASQ.

As the principal of Robitaille Associates, she has helped numerous companies in diverse fields to achieve ISO 9001 registration and to improve their quality management systems. She has conducted training courses for thousands of individuals on such topics as corrective action, management review, auditing, document control, and implementing ISO 9001.

Denise's books include: *The Corrective Action Handbook, The Management Review Handbook, The Preventive Action Handbook, Root Cause Analysis: Basic Tools and Techniques, Document Control,* and *Managing Supplier-Related Processes.* She is a regular columnist for *The Auditor* newsletter and is the author of numerous articles.

www.ingramcontent.com/pod-product-compliance
Lightning Source LLC
Chambersburg PA
CBHW070930270326
41927CB00011B/2805

9 781932 828689